Intimate Love Letters
to the Father

Intimate Love Letters
to the Father
by Stanley Nicole Dolly

Intimate Love Letters to the Father

Trilogy Christian Publishers A Wholly Owned Subsidary of Trinity Broadcasting Network

2442 Michelle Drive Tustin, CA 92780

Rights Department, 2442 Michelle Drive, Tustin, CA 92780.

Trilogy Christian Publishing/TBN and colophon are trademarks of Trinity Broadcasting Network.

For information about special discounts for bulk purchases, please contact Trilogy Christian Publishing.

Trilogy Disclaimer: The views and content expressed in this book are those of the author and may not necessarily reflect the views and doctrine of Trilogy Christian Publishing or the Trinity Broadcasting Network.

Manufactured in the United States of America

10 9 8 7 6 5 4 3 2 1

Library of Congress Cataloging-in-Publication Data is available.

ISBN: 978-1-64773-376-6

E-ISBN: 978-1-64773-377-3

Contents

Dedication

This book is dedicated to my mother, Dr. Patricia Ann Dolly.

From the time of being a young child, I remember my mom trusting Jesus. From the mountains to the valleys and everything in between, she trusted Jesus. She was a single parent with two sassy kids to raise... But, God! Through every struggle and hardship, she trusted Jesus. She had many nights crying in the darkness. The odds were against her...But, God! God had a purpose for this soul.

This soul gave birth to a daughter and a son that love Jesus more than anything. Most parents pray for success for their children, but this woman prayed for our souls! God has predestined me to share His loving and forgiving heart with all. She taught us that God is a God of love! She is a hardworking woman from west Michigan with a plan and a prayer for her children; follow the Lord along with your heart. My mother taught us that God offers love, joy, hope, and peace to every deprived soul.

Love you, Mommy

Foreword

The Word of God can come from many sources; whether from the top of a mountain, through a burning bush, or from the cross. What Stanley Nicole Dolly has done is captured God's Word and presented it to us in yet another way so that we may digest it, give us sustenance, and hope moving forward.

Yes, she comes to us to deliver words of hope! Words... Proverbs 18:21 tells us that both death and life are in the power of the tongue. This text will bring nothing but life to those who open themselves up to it. Hope is the feeling of expectation and desire for a certain thing to happen. What is it for you that can or will change your life today? Matthew 17:20 tells us that if we have enough faith even as small as a mustard seed, we can say to the mountains *move*, and it will move! Nothing will be impossible for you.

Even the tiny word "of" has meaning. It's a preposition that expresses the relationship between a part and a whole. For example, as God's children we are just a part of the whole body of Christ. So the words of hope from this book are just that, small units of speech that express our relationship to God with the feeling and desire for a certain thing to happen. Behold and watch the miracles that are to happen in your life by reading this text. And then suddenly!

God be praised! Peace, power, and love prevail today and always.

Amen

Lloyd C. Crews, PhD

When my father and my mother forsake me,
then the Lord will take me up

—Psalms 27:10 (KJV)

A Day to Rejoice!

God, I praise You, and I lift Your name above all others! I lift Your Word above Your name—a book filled with promises unending!

You have lifted my soul from the deepest of pits. If not for You and Your grace, my life as I know it would be over! But a new day means new hope, new joy, new peace, new choices, fresh attitudes, new smiles, and most of all a new day to bless people and invite them into Your kingdom of unending peace.

You are like a sweet honeycomb or a just-ripe sugar cane! Just to be in Your presence for a second will last a lifetime.

I am filled with Your spirit and Your waters flow in my belly and quench every thirst! Teach me Your ways… Teach me to love the way You love. Teach me to be unselfish; always looking at others needs before my own.

You are a melody in my heart that is unending. Play for me the strings of *love* and peace. My only rest is in Your arms.

I am safe from the world and all of its chaos! Others trust in self-worthiness, education, money, husbands, wives, sugar daddies and mommas…But my trust is in only You!

My only breath is in You! Feed me more and may it overflow in my life.

Oh child of the Most High, rejoice for He alone is worthy!

This is the day the Lord has made; we will rejoice and be glad in it.

—Psalm 118:24

From your thoughts:

Why is your heart rejoicing today?

_____

_____

_____

_____

_____

_____

_____

_____

_____

_____

_____

_____

_____

_____

_____

Your love letter to the Father

I Want to Mirror You

Oh Glorious Father,

I am renewed in Spirit and in strength on this blessed morning. So many souls were lost this weekend yet You spared us.

You must have work for all of the saved souls to complete for the building of Your kingdom. Today, we will make right choices based on God's unmerited grace and favor.

Lord, help us to make choices that mirror You—Your humbleness, Your wisdom, Your patience, and most of all, Your love.

Lord, cover our minds and make them more like You. We will make the daily decision to rejoice in Your goodness.

Peace You leave with us, not as the world gives and takes it away.

Only God gives and never takes away or forsakes.

Rest in me Holy Spirit causing my soul to rest in You; peace beyond understanding.

...and the peace of God, which surpasses all understanding, will guard your hearts and minds through Christ Jesus.

—Philippians 4:7

From your thoughts:

Guard my heart and mind from...

_____

_____

_____

_____

_____

_____

_____

_____

_____

_____

_____

_____

_____

_____

_____

_____

_____

Your love letter to the Father

Dear God

I am thankful for
Your Love
Your blood
Your mercy
Your kindness
How I am able to boldly come to You
How You always provide
How You bless me when I should not be blessed
For my fabulous job
For my fabulous family
Infinite possibilities

And God said to Moses, "I AM WHO I AM." And He said, "Thus you shall say to the children of Israel, 'I AM has sent me to you.'"

—Exodus 3:14

From your thoughts:

God you are to me...

_____

_____

_____

_____

_____

_____

_____

_____

_____

_____

_____

_____

_____

_____

_____

_____

_____

Your love letter to the Father

Hello My Love

Hello my Love! I have missed You so much!
I long for Your touch in the morning!
You have demanded the sun to shine on all of Your chil-
dren—offering hope!
How could You love this people?
How could You love me?
Your grace surpasses all that I can imagine
You are my only hope
All that I need is in You

It is a new day for me

I am… such a special soul
I am… such a light in the midst of darkness
I am… such a mess
I am healed from my worst weapon… which is myself

I have such a heart that loves and seeks her Father
But there is good news… I know that You hear me and
You always understand
I will not rest until I see the Presence of God

And by His Word, I am made perfect!

just as He chose us in Him before the foundation of the world, that we should be holy and without blame before Him in love

—Ephesians 1:4

From your thoughts:

He knew you and chose you anyway...

_____

_____

_____

_____

_____

_____

_____

_____

_____

_____

_____

_____

_____

_____

_____

Your love letter to the Father

Period the End

Lord my God!
Rejoice!
It is all about You!
I cherish You with all my heart
I see the me You see!
I know that You have prepared a path for the unrighteous
I love You and Your grace is sufficient
This is a life changing day
I will take time to hear Your voice
Not in passing, but deliberately
Taking the time to hear You and show my desperation
Thank You for Your favor, protection, provision and
    most of all Your love
I love You and the freedom You give me!
I will give my life to You for Your control

Period the End!

So when Jesus had received the sour wine, He said, "It is finished!" And bowing His head, He gave up His spirit.

—John 19:30

From your thoughts:

Declare what is finished

_____

_____

_____

_____

_____

_____

_____

_____

_____

_____

_____

_____

_____

_____

_____

_____

_____

Your love letter to the Father

My Destiny

Lord, I first come to You with praise and thanksgiving
For You are truly the great I am!
I thank You for Your precious unblemished Son, who
    sits next to You on the throne of glory
I also give all my thanks to the Comforter that Your Son
    left for us—the beautiful quieting Holy Spirit
Lord, I submit my will for Yours and I say Yes to where
    I am and where I am about to go
I fully trust Your will and perfect love
I will constantly be mindful of "by your patience possess
    your souls" (Luke 21:19).
I know in my heart that You have predestined me before the foun-
    dations of the earth to do a great work in Your kingdom
All that I am I dedicate to You
Everything I will become I place in Your outstretched arm
Only Your arm is able to contain my destination
All my heart, love and soul… I give

Eternal love

> For I know the thoughts that I think toward you, says the LORD, thoughts of peace and not of evil, to give you a future and a hope.
>
> —Jeremiah 29:11

From your thoughts:

Write your God given destiny

_____

_____

_____

_____

_____

_____

_____

_____

_____

_____

_____

_____

_____

_____

_____

_____

Your love letter to the Father

A Mother's Heart

A mother's heart was created by none other than our
heavenly Father!

Only He could create a heart that knows no end of the
road called love

Only the Father could give you more than enough tears
to cry and smiles that will last for eternity... on that
long journey called motherhood!

Only the Father could create the beauty in grandchil-
dren, born and those to come!

A mother's heart is made of jewels—diamonds, rubies,
gems, and only the finest of the roughest yet valu-
able stones

The stones that can't be broken

Only a mother would travel to ends of the earth on hot
coals... bare feet, complaining, and yelling all the way

Yet, she is determined to make it happen

Only a mother gets a call in the middle of the night
and says, "I will give my house and all that I have to
release my son or daughter from prison, if just for a
moment..."

Only a mother's heart is as deep as the ocean and that
heart is God's greatest gift!

God bless all mothers!

You deserve the world in your back pocket and in your
fancy red-bottom shoes

When Jesus therefore saw His mother, and the disciple whom He loved standing by, He said to His mother, "Woman, behold your son!" Then He said to the disciple, "Behold your mother!" And from that hour that disciple took her to his own home.

—John 19:26–27

From your thoughts:

Behold your mother...

_____

_____

_____

_____

_____

_____

_____

_____

_____

_____

_____

_____

_____

_____

_____

_____

Your love letter to the Father

A Taste of Your Love

Oh, how sweet is the taste of Your love
My soul quivers at the thought of Your touch
My heart springs water unending
I remain in awe at Your love and understanding
The sun is shining over me at all times
I am hedged in by Your mercies, grace, favor and the
    tallest wall of all—love

Only You are able to make me the woman of God that
    I was put on this earth to be.

All the days of my life…
I will always put You first
I will be used by You in every way
I will make a difference
I will love
I will laugh
I will show mercy
I will serve
I will help
I will feed
I will shelter
I will forgive
I will walk in peace
I will walk in joy
I will walk in You

Forever Your child

Behold, how good and how pleasant it is.
For brethren to dwell together in unity! It
is like the precious oil upon the head, running
down on the beard of Aaron...

—Psalms 133:1–2

From your thoughts:

Soak in the precious oil of the Lord

_____

_____

_____

_____

_____

_____

_____

_____

_____

_____

_____

_____

_____

_____

Your love letter to the Father

My Lord and Savior!

I am so eternally grateful for Your loving kindness!
You are a sovereign King!
How lovely it is to dwell in Your Presence!
In You I breathe, live, and am able!
You have placed my feet on solid ground… I am walk-
    ing on clouds
Almighty, powerful, miracle worker, healer… my heart
I love You and will forever bask in Your love!
Your name is high above the heavens and every breath-
    ing being
Whisper to me and breathe life into this lifeless body
Offer us hope in our seemingly hopeless situations
Thank You Lord for making a way for Your children
Thank You for Your never ending supply of miracles
    that You perform daily
You are the air that I breathe and the joy in my spirit
You are the love in my heart.
I rejoice in Your goodness
Speak, oh Holy One of Israel

I am listening for Your direction

For unto us a Child is born, unto us a Son is given; And the government will be upon His shoulder. And His name will be called Wonderful, Counselor, Mighty God, Everlasting Father, Prince of Peace.

—Isaiah 9:6

Journal your thoughts:

What has Jesus birth done for you?

_____

_____

_____

_____

_____

_____

_____

_____

_____

_____

_____

_____

_____

_____

_____

_____

_____

_____

Your love letter to the Father

America

America... who are you... deep within your soul

The nation is terrified about where we are headed

Disease, devastation, hate, despair, unemployment, lost heroes, loneliness, and mask for all

Yet, we are one nation under God indivisible with liberty and justice for all!

Indivisible means incapable or impossible of being divided

God has called His people to trust in His infinite wisdom and love

When men came to devour our flesh, they stumbled and fell

God is always the same.. today, yesterday and forever

COVID-19 is a devastating virus for the human race

But, God—Your eternal Father has all power in His hands

We will trust in the Lord with all of our hearts

We will not try to understand this madness

Lord, we will acknowledge You, and allow You to direct our paths

After the dust settles and the sun continues to rise early

America, your path is this

God is and will always remain on the throne!

He has called America to walk fearless in love, peace, and inclusiveness

God called America to refuse the idea of hatred of any person or living being

We are to walk and remain in His image; regardless of what this world brings

America, hold your head high and stand fearless against
the unknown
I am my brother's keeper
God created the heavens and the earth, with a whisper
All–powerful Omnificent… creating all things and
having unlimited power of creation
And the history book ends with this
Peace be still and wait on the Lord

He will turn America's mourning into dancing. I say,
wait on the Lord
Selah

Yea, though I walk through the valley of the shadow of death, I will fear no evil; For You are with me; Your rod and Your staff, they comfort me

—Psalms 23:4

Journal your thoughts:

Write a tribute to our fallen Heroes and First Responders

Your love letter to the Father

My Sustainer

Lord, You are my *everything*!

My sustainer in a world of darkness!

I am able to be confident in Your ever presence and Your power

Though I am low, You are *high*!

You lift me out of the pit as my forefather David wrote in the book of Psalms

When I am at my lowest point, You lift me up

You remind me that I am only a mere mortal and without You, I am nothing!

I meditate on Your works and Your many blessings

From Sun up to sun set, You reign on high!

I love the sound of Your sovereign name

JESUS, as I call in the midst of trouble

As the tears flow, there is solace in the name above all names

Sovereign means possessing supreme or ultimate power

There is none like You! JESUS... I call Your name

JESUS, all evil flees

JESUS! JESUS! JESUS!

My only Sustainer!

How precious also are Your thoughts to me, O God! How great is the sum of them! If I should count them, they would be more in number than the sand; When I awake, I am still with You.

—Psalms 139:17–18

Journal your thoughts:

What is the largest trial God has sustained you through?

_____

_____

_____

_____

_____

_____

_____

_____

_____

_____

_____

_____

_____

_____

Your love letter to the Father

Today

Today...one of God's children was diagnosed with terminal brain cancer

Today...one of God's children buried their own child

Today...a young teen, with a promising future, took his own life due to cyber bullying

Today...our Country is unjustly divided by the colors of red and blue

Today...a child is missing

Today...we are plagued by a deadly virus

Today...in a moment, your life could be changed forever

But God...

Today...I will rejoice that I have You as my Savior

Today...I will enjoy His gifts of family, love and friends

Today...I will not worry about tomorrow

Today...I will rest in Your bosom

Today... I will be thankful for each moment

Today...Your grace is sufficient.

And He said to me, "My grace is sufficient for you, for My strength is made perfect in weakness." Therefore, most gladly I will rather boast in my infirmities, that the power of Christ may rest upon me.

—2 Corinthians 12:9

Journal your thoughts:
What is your heart anxious about today that God's grace is sufficient for?

_____

_____

_____

_____

_____

_____

_____

_____

_____

_____

_____

_____

_____

_____

_____

_____

Your love letter to the Father

Daddy

I wanted to take some time out of my day to render up
   praises and thanksgiving devotion for there is none
   like You!
So high and mighty, You can't be seen or understood
Your blessings seem to flow like a never-ending river
   without a bottom
I can't express to You the love and gratefulness that exist
   in my heart
A heart that You made only for me
Every heart is different and unique in Your eyes
None of Your children love You the same... though
   there are billions!
You have created in us a unique and peculiar heart with
   Your love inside each and every one
No smile is the same
No love is the same
No praise is the same
No story is the same
Yet, You know all things
Wow, what an amazing God we serve!
You hear the prayers of Your sorrowful children
Though sorrowful from the world
But filled with the joy of Your love
And the promised eternal resting place, You have pre-
   pared for us
Lord, help me to be a work in Your hands
Show me how to bless others with the only love that is
   perfect!

Reveal Yourself in me

Forever Your clay

And Jabez called on the God of Israel saying, "Oh, that You would bless me indeed, and enlarge my territory, that Your hand would be with me, and that You would keep me from evil, that I may not cause pain!" So God granted him what he requested.

—1 Chronicles 4:10

Journal your thoughts:
What does your enlarged territory look like?

_____

_____

_____

_____

_____

_____

_____

_____

_____

_____

_____

_____

_____

_____

_____

_____

Your love letter to the Father

Do You Know Your Worth?

I am a giant of God kicking down barriers in His kingdom!
I am trampling over the serpent and all of his lies
I have a heart made with jewels and a never ending
 resource of love
I am a prayer warrior and intercessor as the Holy
 Spirit leads
I can see my future and nothing about it is ordinary
Ask me why?
I am a daughter of the Most High King!
He created the waters, hills, valleys and all of the earth
The atmosphere belongs to my Daddy
He has promised to restore everything that I lost, and
 multiply it by at least double!
Every tear that I shed
Every sleepless night
Every anxiety attack
Every broken relationship
Every closed door
Every untruth
Every lie the devil told me about myself, my family and
 my future
Have disappeared into the sea of the lost!

Today is the first day of the rest of my life
I see the sun and a path made with the brightest
 future ever
I am a blessing to all those that grace my path
Not because of me, but because of You!

For You formed my inward parts; You covered me in my mother's womb. I will praise You, for I am fearfully and wonderfully made; marvelous are Your works, and that my soul knows very well.

—Psalms 139:14

Journal your thoughts:

Before the foundations of the earth… You were made perfect…

_____

_____

_____

_____

_____

_____

_____

_____

_____

_____

_____

_____

_____

_____

_____

Your love letter to the Father

Jesus I Need You More

Jesus, I need You more
More than a hungry soul needs food
More than a bird needs to fly
More than an ocean needs water
More than a person needs oxygen
More than an infant needs to be nurtured
More than a singer needs to sing
More than a poet needs to write
More than a tear needs to cry
More than a rain drop needs a cloud
More than winter needs snow
More than spring needs flowers
More than a politician needs politics
More than a lover needs love
More than a sky needs blue

And more than a desperate soul needs saving

I need You more than life itself
Without You there is no me

Lord, I need You more

Jesus answered and said to her, "If you knew the gift of God, and who it is who says to you, 'Give Me a drink,' you would have asked Him, and He would have given you living water."

—John 4:10

Journal your thoughts:

Rest at the well with Jesus…

_____

_____

_____

_____

_____

_____

_____

_____

_____

_____

_____

_____

_____

_____

_____

Your love letter to the Father

Monday Blues Changed to Monday Morning Praise

Dear Daddy,
Thank You for this day
For we shall rejoice and be made glad in it
Today, unlike billions of others around the world
I find myself working for an excellent wage
My children and family members are safe and sound
Everyone is accounted for
Though my dreams were dark
The sun still rose early this morning

Your blood is just as red and forgiving as it was
Two thousand years ago

I am still a descendant of Kings
My seed is still blessed
My sins are still cast in the lake of forgiveness
Never to be seen again
My heart still yearns for Your love and presence
And my hope will never perish
Because, I am Your child
Monday morning blues changed

You have turned for me my mourning into dancing; You have put off my sackcloth and clothed me with gladness, to the end that my glory may sing praise to You and not be silent. O LORD my God, I will give thanks to You forever.

—Psalm 30:11–12

Journal your thoughts:

What sackcloth are you taking off today?

_____

_____

_____

_____

_____

_____

_____

_____

_____

_____

_____

_____

_____

_____

_____

_____

Your love letter to the Father

Peace

I am renewed in Spirit and in strength on this blessed morning

So many souls were lost this COVID-19 season; yet You have spared us.

You must have a work for all of the saved souls to complete in the building of Your kingdom

Today, we will make right choices based on God's unmerited grace and favor

Lord, help us to make choices that mirror You

Your humbleness

Your wisdom

Your patience

Most of all, Your love!

Lord, cover our minds and make them more like You!

We will make the decision to *rejoice* in Your goodness

Peace You leave with us... not as the world gives and takes away

Only God gives and never takes away or forsakes

Rest in me Holy Spirit causing my soul to rest in You... peace beyond all understanding

Let us therefore be diligent to enter that rest, lest anyone fall according to the same example of disobedience. For the word of God is living and powerful, and sharper than any two-edged sword, piercing even to the division of soul and spirit, and of joints and marrow, and is a discerner of the thoughts and intents of the heart.

—Hebrews 4:11–12

Journal your thoughts:

What does your soul need rest from today?

_____

_____

_____

_____

_____

_____

_____

_____

_____

_____

_____

_____

_____

_____

_____

Your love letter to the Father

Hello, My Peace Maker

The love larger than eternity!
One moment in Your arms is like an eternity of peace!
Slow down my Spirit, God
Let my focus and thanksgiving be totally mindful of the
    sacrifice You have made just for me
I want to describe an emotion greater than love
As I ponder on Your Word
You said that the greatest of these is love
You are love, and there is none greater than You!
I walk in You, and Your kingdom is unending
Your spirit surrounds me and covers me at all times
I walk in Your unending favor and peace
I am walking on rainbows
May I love people into Your kingdom; for You have
    wooed me back into Your loving arms
I was so far away
Like an inner tube drifting into the middle of an end-
    less ocean
Though my heart did not know a way back to You
A life line and life jacket were thrown out to me; to save
    my life
I thought that I was too far to return, but You reminded me
"Nothing is impossible with You" (see Luke 1:37).
May I become like You on this earth
I need to be a light in a world of darkness, offering love
    and providing fruit for Your people
You have expanded my territory and my responsibility
Open my ears and heart to Your perfect will

Thank You for drowning out the noise of the world

How do I say with words *thank you* for Your unblemished Son

I don't say it with words, I become it with deeds

Deeds and duties of building Your kingdom, which is the highest calling!

Fill me up, Lord so I can overflow with Your Shekinah Glory!

I love You, Daddy!

You are my first love

You called me to be a warrior and a world changer!

Thank You for Your abilities and authority that You placed in me

I will live humbly with total dependence on You for every breath!

Eternity is waiting

The Cross saved me—Yes, even me!

Be anxious for nothing, but in everything by prayer and supplication, with thanksgiving, let your requests be made known to God; and the peace of God, which surpasses all understanding, will guard your hearts and minds through Christ Jesus

—Philippians 4:6–7

Journal your thoughts:

The war is over...

_____

_____

_____

_____

_____

_____

_____

_____

_____

_____

_____

_____

_____

_____

_____

_____

Your love letter to the Father

Lord, How I Love and Trust Thee

Lord, how I love Thee!
You bring peace to my chaotic mind
You give joy to my desperate and sorrowful heart
You give hope in every hopeless situation
Your favors are unending
I am a child of the Most High God and He will always
    love and protect me
He has only the very best for me and nothing less will do!
The more I know about You, the more I loathe myself…
    show me who You see!
I know that I can be the person You created me to be
But never without You, and only because of You never fail!
Take this anxiety from me and cover me with Your
    boldness!
Erase from me the pain of my past
Except to remember how praise worthy You are
And how far You have carried me

I want to be like You!
I long to feel Your touch in the morning!
One kiss
One touch
And my heart will burn forever!

I love You, I love You, I love You, I love You!

being confident of this very thing, that He who has begun a good work in you will complete it until the day of Jesus Christ

—Philippians 1:6

Journal your thoughts:

What good work is God completing in you?

_____

_____

_____

_____

_____

_____

_____

_____

_____

_____

_____

_____

_____

_____

_____

_____

Your love letter to the Father

Lord, Hallowed Be Thy Name

Lord, hallowed be Your name!
The only name I know, my God, Lord, Savior, Sustainer,
    Provider, Miracle Worker
All that I am, I dedicate to You
I am nothing without You
But, with You, I can do all things
How can I ever thank you enough for all You do for
    me; lowly, disgusting, dirty and not worthy? But then
    there was the blood of Jesus
My Redeemer

I am not confused.
All blessings flow from You!
I will walk with You all the days of my life!
Thank You for the hedge of protection!
I love You with my whole heart!
My love, eternal!

In this manner, therefore, pray: Our Father in heaven, hallowed be Your name. Your kingdom come. Your will be done on earth as it is in heaven.

—Matthew 6:9–10

Journal your thoughts:

Hallowed means made holy; consecrated, greatly revered and honored...

_____

_____

_____

_____

_____

_____

_____

_____

_____

_____

_____

_____

_____

Your love letter to the Father

Lord, Rest My Roaring Soul

Dearest Father,
My soul is yearning for You this morning
My soul is in the darkest of pits
There is no relief from the anxiety in my mind
Why can't I just focus on the end that You have prepared for me?
For only You know the plans that are prepared just for me
Wrap Your arms around me and never let me go
Tell me You have already given me the desires of my heart
All I have to do is wait until morning when the dew hits the grass
May I crawl in Your lap and hear the fairytale that begins with me and ends
Happily ever after

Lord, rest my restless soul

Peace I leave with you, My peace I give to you; not as the world gives do I give to you. Let not your heart be troubled, neither let it be afraid.

—John 14:27

Journal your thoughts:

What does your peace look like?

_____

_____

_____

_____

_____

_____

_____

_____

_____

_____

_____

_____

_____

_____

_____

_____

Your love letter to the Father

God Has Supplied All of My Needs

He has supplied all of my needs!
And my God has supplied all of my needs according to
    His riches and glory!
I will not doubt what God says in His word
What He has said in His Word is
I am spiritual
I am smart
I am beautiful
I am resourceful
And most of all
I am loved by my Father
He has anointed me to be a change agent in the atmo-
    sphere around me!
I will not die, but I will live
And be the God fearing woman that only He could
    create me to be.
I am honest
I am loving
I am trustworthy
I am always smiling because God's glowing light shines
    on me
I share that light with others both Jews and Gentiles!
I am chosen and everything that I touch prospers
God is even making a path for me as I think and speak
The path is made with jewels and every beautiful thing

And my God shall supply all your need according to His riches in glory by Christ Jesus. Now to our God and Father be glory forever and ever. Amen.

—Philippians 4:19-20

Journal your thoughts:

What need can God supply for you that only a miracle working God can supply?

_____

_____

_____

_____

_____

_____

_____

_____

_____

_____

_____

_____

_____

_____

_____

_____

Your love letter to the Father

The Perfect Transition

Death is a part of life
Just as the seasons change.
The will of God is unquestioned
Live each day in truth
Live each day with thanksgiving
The grass was once green
But is now thrown in the fire
Mourn for the living
And not the dead in Christ
For the children of Christ shall reign eternally
The sweet taste of death
Otherwise known as
The perfect transition
Bow down to God's perfect and timeless will

For whoever desires to save his life will lose it, but whoever loses his life for My sake will find it.

—Matthew 16:25

Journal your thoughts:
Though I grieve... I rejoice...

_____

_____

_____

_____

_____

_____

_____

_____

_____

_____

_____

_____

_____

_____

_____

_____

Your letter to the Father

Your Majesty

I am not sure why You love me the way that You do
My natural mind can't conceive why You continue to
   provide for me
Lord
Your Majesty
You *always* come through for Your children
Words cannot express
How You continue to love me
Words cannot express
How You continue to provide for me
All You do is in spite of my own wretchedness
I love You
My heart sings to You
Thank You for always taking care of Your children!
You blow my mind into the heavens
Beam me up Lord

Always
Forever in love
With Your Majesty

In the year that King Uzziah died, I saw the Lord sitting on a throne, high and lifted up, and the train of His robe filled the temple. Above it stood seraphim; each one had 6 wings; with two he covered his face, with two he covered his feet; with two he flew. And one cried to another said: Holy, holy, holy is the Lord of Host; the whole earth is full of his glory!"

—Isaiah 6:1–3

Journal your thoughts:

Magnify the majestic God with me...

_____

_____

_____

_____

_____

_____

_____

_____

_____

_____

_____

_____

_____

_____

_____

_____

Your love letter to the Father

Let the Church Say, Amen

I am!
I am a woman of God
I am a worshiper of the Lord
I am a woman with a heart filled with goodness, kind-
   ness, and mercy
I am a beautiful gorgeous girl (God says so)
I am curvy and shapely like my ancestors
I am a woman with a servant's heart
I am a woman with a giving spirit
I am a woman who loves her family
I am a woman willing to make sacrifices for others
I am a woman who refuses to complain
I am a woman thankful for all God has provided
I am a good steward over all that God has blessed me with
I am the righteousness of God… given by His grace!

Let the church say, Amen!

Charm is deceitful and beauty is passing, but a woman who fears the LORD, she shall be praised. Give her of the fruit of her hands, and let her own works praise her in the gates.

—Proverbs 31:30–31

Journal your thoughts:
What can we learn from the Proverbs 31 woman?

_____

_____

_____

_____

_____

_____

_____

_____

_____

_____

_____

_____

_____

Your letter to the Father

In God I Trust

I trust You Lord, my God!
The Father of all nations
The Light of my world
You have created me from dust
You have designed my heart and soul for Your perfect will
You walk with me through every challenge
You lift me higher than the clouds
You carry me through every victory
My God offers peace in every situation
Because I trust in You... I am filled with faith
Because I trust in You... I have love for my neighbor
I walk in boldness
Nothing is able to stand against me
Because I trust in You... I am walking in my promised
    destiny
Trusting You allows favor to flow in my life
Your abundance flows like the Jordan River in every
    area in my life
You have ravished my heart only to make it whole
I trust You to take my broken, desperate pieces
And mold them into Your hands and feet on this earth
I am letting go of it all
I am landing safely in Your arms
Free falling into the hands of the Savior

"Be strong and of good courage, do not fear nor be afraid of them; for the LORD your God, He is the One who goes with you. He will not leave you nor forsake you."

—Deuteronomy 31:6

Journal your thoughts:
What are you trusting God for today?

_____

_____

_____

_____

_____

_____

_____

_____

_____

_____

_____

_____

_____

_____

Your letter to the Father

Your Promises to Keep

My dear sweet Lord
Today is a day full of hope and promises to keep
I am left safe and sound in Your loving arms of refuge
    and protection
Your love for me is deeper than any river or ocean
Your word says
"When I awake… I am still with You" (Psalm 139:18).
Thank You for the eternal gift of Your love
Not judging… just giving Your gift to all
My soul is at peace in and with You
All of my needs are met and I am walking in abundance
Spiritually, I am whole!
All my sins are forgiven!
A new life is mine!
You light up my life!
My only hope is in You!
You are a love
My only love

A thousand may fall at your side and ten thousand at your right hand; but it shall not come near you. Only with your eyes shall you look, and see the reward of the wicked.

—Psalms 91:7–8

Journal your thoughts:
God, You have promised to keep me...

_____

_____

_____

_____

_____

_____

_____

_____

_____

_____

_____

_____

_____

_____

_____

_____

Your love letter to the Father

Yesterday Erased

To the only one I adore
Yesterday, I chose to focus on my needs, wants, and self-
ish desires
The road that leads to a bottomless pit
A deep well without water.
Constant worry, addictions, unrighteousness, greed,
malice for my neighbor
Jealousy and self-destruction
A road clearly not chosen for Your children

But today
My mind is set on You, oh my sweet love
You woke me up this morning with love in Your heart!
You kissed me on the forehead and whispered, *come away
with me, my love*
You clothed and fed me
You offered a wise road to travel
The road without lack, worry, sickness, anxiety, pain,
distress and dreadful thoughts of tomorrow!
You offered a road filled with joy, peace, and protection
from all things!
A road that allows me to be a blessing to all those I encounter
A road that allows me to show Your love, mercy, and grace
A road that reveals Your hidden secrets in Your kingdom

I am a child of the "Most High God," and I am *free* from
the world and its cares
Everywhere that the soles of my feet touch shall prosper!
I am anointed to preach the good news of the gospel.
I am chosen for such a time as this
Oh, Lord, shine Your light through me
Make me Your vessel!
I will walk in Your path and not the one that Satan has
designed

"The Spirit of the LORD is upon Me because He has anointed Me to preach the gospel to the poor; He has sent Me to heal the brokenhearted, to proclaim liberty to the captives, and recovery of sight to the blind; To set at liberty those who are oppressed; to proclaim the acceptable year of the LORD."

—Luke 4:18–19

Journal your thoughts:
God has anointed me to...

_____

_____

_____

_____

_____

_____

_____

_____

_____

_____

_____

_____

_____

_____

_____

_____

Your love letter to the Father

My Confession and God's Covenant

My confession and God's covenant

I am living free of sickness and disease

I am free from poverty, lack, sexual immorality, sin, and anything apart from the Word of God! This is my confession and God's covenant

I will not accept anything less for myself and my family

All of those that hinder me God has removed from my sight and path

I am not moved by anything

I am only lead by the Holy Spirit and the root of everything I do is love

Love not as the world gives it

But as God died on the cross—Love

I will love my neighbor and enemies as God loves me without fault and consequence

Just pure unadulterated love!

And may the Most High God, the only God—the Ruler, Counselor, Wonderful, Almighty, Everlasting Father says it is so!

"The LORD will command the blessing on you in your storehouses and in all to which you set your hand, and He will bless you in the land which the LORD your God is giving you. The LORD will establish you as a holy people to Himself, just as He has sworn to you, if you keep the commandments of the LORD your God and walk in His ways."

—Deuteronomy 28:8–9

Journal your thoughts:
My confession...

_____

_____

_____

_____

_____

_____

_____

_____

_____

_____

_____

_____

_____

_____

Your love letter to the Father

Victory

God we come before You with
All honor
All praise
You have given me the name Victory before the foundations of the earth
I am Victory
Victorious in all things
Inheritance—I have inherited a land flowing with milk
and honey
Christ–like
Triumphant—Sound the trumpets
Obedient to God's word
Righteous—I am the Righteousness of God
Yahweh—The only one that makes us victorious

When I know who You are
Only then can I begin to see who I am
I am made victorious in You
Lord
The things in my life that were once so large
Have become small
Because I am victorious in You
I will praise You in advance for the victory

Then Jerubbaal (that is Gideon) and all the people who were with him rose early and encamped beside the well of Harod, so that the camp of the Midianites was on the north side of them by the hill of Moreh in the valley. And the Lord said to Gideon, "The people who are with you are too many for Me to give the Midianites into their hands, lest Israel claim glory for itself against Me, saying, 'My own hand has saved me.'"

—Judges 7:1–2

Journal your thoughts:
My victory is totally dependent on You Lord.

_____

_____

_____

_____

_____

_____

_____

_____

_____

_____

_____

_____

_____

_____

_____

Your love letter to the Father

Fear No Evil

God has not called us to live in fear
If you let it
Fear
Will steal your life
Fear
The dread of tomorrow
If I decide to live in fear, where would it end?
Every time I get into the car my heart would tremble
I would be tortured by every phone call… waiting for
the bad news
A plane ride would never be the same
Instead of the glory in the clouds
I would see only a black box used to figure out what
went wrong
The white coat from the doctor's office would become
a nightmare
A virus or germ might come home with me and cost me
my life
And then in 2020 there was COVID–19
My worst fears came true

God deliver my fearful heart

Please help my unbelief
I refuse to let fear take over my earthly life
For Your promise says
Fear no evil
I release fear in my life today
I will chose to trust You over fear
I will chose Your Word over my thoughts
I will fear no evil

> Because you have made the lord, who is my refuge, even the most high, your dwelling place, no evil shall befall you, nor shall any plaque come near your dwelling

> —Psalms 91:9–10

Journal your thoughts:
I will fear no evil

_____

_____

_____

_____

_____

_____

_____

_____

_____

_____

_____

_____

_____

_____

Your love letter to the Father

Abba Father

Abba Father
You are not stained
You are filled with glory
I cry out with a child like heart, Abba Father
Abba Father
I surrender to you completely
With total dependability
Like a child nursing from his handmaid
Feed me Daddy
I thirst and hunger for Your touch
Feed me until my soul is full
Feed me so that I can spill over into my neighbors tea
My soul rest in my Abba Father
And Your glory fills the temple
You have made me Your temple
This world will make you seek refuge
Abba Father, my refuge is You

Abba Father…
Abba Father…
Abba Father…

And because you are sons, God has sent forth the Spirit of his son into your hearts, crying out "Abba Father!" Therefore you were no longer a slave but son, and if a son, then an heir of God through Christ

—Galatians 4:6

Journal your thoughts:
Abba Father...

_____

_____

_____

_____

_____

_____

_____

_____

_____

_____

_____

_____

_____

_____

_____

_____

_____

Your love letter to the Father